MYTHICAL UNICORNS

FANTASY CREATURES

Gareth Stevens PUBLISHING

HOT TOPICS

BENJAMIN PROUDFIT

Please visit our website, www.garethstevens.com. For a free color catalog of all our high-quality books, call toll free 1-800-542-2595 or fax 1-877-542-2596.

Library of Congress Cataloging-in-Publication Data
Names: Proudfit, Benjamin.
Title: Mythical unicorns / Benjamin Proudfit.
Description: Buffalo, NY : Gareth Stevens Publishing, 2026. | Series: Fantasy creatures | Includes glossary and index.
Identifiers: ISBN 9781482475333 (pbk.) | ISBN 9781482475340 (library bound) | ISBN 9781482475357 (ebook)
Subjects: LCSH: Food allergy in children–Juvenile literature.
Classification: LCC P93 2026 | DDC –dc23

Published in 2026 by
Gareth Stevens Publishing
2544 Clinton Street
Buffalo, NY 14224

Designer: Leslie Taylor
Editor: Kristen Nelson

Photo credits: Cover (unicorn), pp. 1, 11, 25 Shutterstock AI Generator/Shutterstock.com; cover and series art (neon circle) Ikrill/Shutterstock.com, (rough frame) TarnishArt/Shutterstock.com, (splotchy background) TiffanyShanks/Shutterstock.com; p. 5 Maximilian100/Shutterstock.com; p. 7 Kizel Cotiw-an/Shutterstock.com; p. 9 (woodcut) Dodge Fund, 1949/Shutterstock.com, (stamp) File:Stamp seal and modern impression- unicorn and incense burner (?) MET DP23101 (cropped).jpg_commons.wikimedia.org, (Iran unicorn) Mohammad.m.nazari/ File:Unicorn in Apadana, Shush, Iran–2017-10.jpg_commons.wikimedia.org; p. 13 ANN_UDOD/Shutterstock.com; p. 15 steve estvanik/Shutterstock.com; p. 17 SergeBertasiusPhotography/Shutterstock.com; p. 19 National Portrait Gallery/File:Darnley stage 3.jpg_commons.wikimedia.org; p. 21 Dr. Kristin Laidre, Polar Science Center, UW NOAA/OAR/OER/File:Pod Monodon monoceros.jpg_commons.wikimedia.org; p. 23 makasana photo/Shutterstock.com; p. 27 Album/Alamy.com; p. 30 (upper left) Sodacan/File:Royal Coat of Arms of the Kingdom of Scotland.svg_commons.wikimedia.org, (upper right) Dgp4004/File:Coat of arms of the United Kingdom (Queen Victoria, lesser arms).svg_commons.wikimedia.org, (middle) Prefeitura de Sorocaba/File:BandeiraSorocaba.svg_commons.wikimedia.org, (lower left) Popadius/File:BandeiraSorocaba.svg_commons.wikimedia.org, (lower right) Great Brightstar/File:Flag of the President of Lithuania (3-5).svg_commons.wikimedia.org.

Printed in China

CPSIA compliance information: Batch #QWGS26: For further information contact Gareth Stevens, at 1-800-542-2595.

CONTENTS

Unicorn Crazy!

Unicorns have been a part of **fantasy** books, movies, and shows for many years. They are part of **pop culture** too. You can buy unicorn stuffies, stickers, T-shirts, and so much more. This interest isn't new—people have been into unicorns for thousands of years!

IMAGINE THAT!

THE "UNI" IN UNICORN MEANS ONE. THE WORD ITSELF TELLS ABOUT THE CREATURE'S ONE HORN!

From Way Back

Mythical unicorn-like creatures have been written about since **ancient** times. They appear in early art from Mesopotamia. An ancient Greek historian wrote of one such animal around 400 BCE. However, it was likely he had seen an Indian rhinoceros!

IMAGINE THAT!

SOME EARLY WRITINGS AND IMAGES OF UNICORNS MAY HAVE BEEN OF AN ANIMAL CALLED AN AUROCHS. THIS WILD COW USED TO LIVE IN EUROPE, NORTH AFRICA, AND ASIA.

Early Unicorn Stories

At first, stories of unicorns said it may have feet like an elephant and the body of a deer. The horn on its head was said to be black or red. Other tales told of a creature with the body of a goat. Later, in European tales, unicorns started to have the body of a horse.

IMAGINE THAT!

SOME WRITERS SAID UNICORNS WERE WHITE. OTHERS SAID THEY WERE YELLOW, RED, OR BROWN.

17TH CENTURY WOODCUT OF A UNICORN

WINGED BULL "UNICORN" FROM ANCIENT CITY IN IRAN

UNICORN IMPRESSION FROM A STAMP MADE CA. 2000 BCE

One well-known European folktale tells of a young woman waiting under a tree for a unicorn. The animal comes to her. It lays its head in her lap. But she's helping hunters who want to catch the unicorn. Later, the woman thinks she sees the unicorn get away!

IMAGINE THAT!

ONE COMMON FEATURE IN UNICORN STORIES IS THAT THE CREATURES ARE VERY HARD TO CATCH.

Asian myths include unicorns too. In Chinese stories, unicorns are called the qilin. They have the body of a deer but shiny, dragon-like scales. Some stories say the qilin has one horn, but others give it two or three horns.

IMAGINE THAT!

A QILIN IS SAID TO BE AN OMEN, OR SOMETHING THAT TELLS OF WHAT IS TO COME.

QILIN

Reports of unicorns continued into the Middle Ages (500–1500). The explorer Marco Polo wrote around the year 1300 about animals he thought were unicorns. He said they had hair like a buffalo and rolled around in mud! Polo had likely seen rhinoceroses.

IMAGINE THAT!

UNICORNS APPEARED IN ART DURING THE MIDDLE AGES. **TAPESTRIES** KNOWN AS "THE LADY AND THE UNICORN" WERE MADE AROUND 1500.

Real or Not?

Into the mid-1550s and early 1600s, people still believed unicorns were real animals. Around this time, they were included in a book about all the animals in the world. By the 1700s, the belief that unicorns truly **existed** had mostly ended.

IMAGINE THAT!

AN ANCIENT ROMAN WRITER INCLUDED UNICORNS IN A BOOK OF ANIMALS TOO. IN MANY PLACES, UNICORNS WERE BOTH MYTH AND FACT FOR A LONG TIME.

Magical Horn

Interest in unicorn horns came about because of the magical stories about it. Horns were said to have healing powers. Stories told of horns making people stay young. Cups made of unicorn horn had great value to important people. They were supposed to counteract poison!

QUEEN ELIZABETH I

IMAGINE THAT!

THE QUEEN OF ENGLAND HAD A "UNICORN HORN" IN THE 1500S. IT WAS WORTH AS MUCH AS A CASTLE!

The "unicorn horns" used in the past often belonged to a large ocean mammal: the narwal. Its long **spiral** tusk gave unicorn horns the look they still have today in art and movies. Modern pictures most often show this horn on a pure white horse.

IMAGINE THAT!

IN THE MID-1660S, DENMARK'S KING HAD A THRONE MADE FROM UNICORN HORN. IN TRUTH, IT WAS MADE OF NARWAL TUSK.

NARWAL TUSK

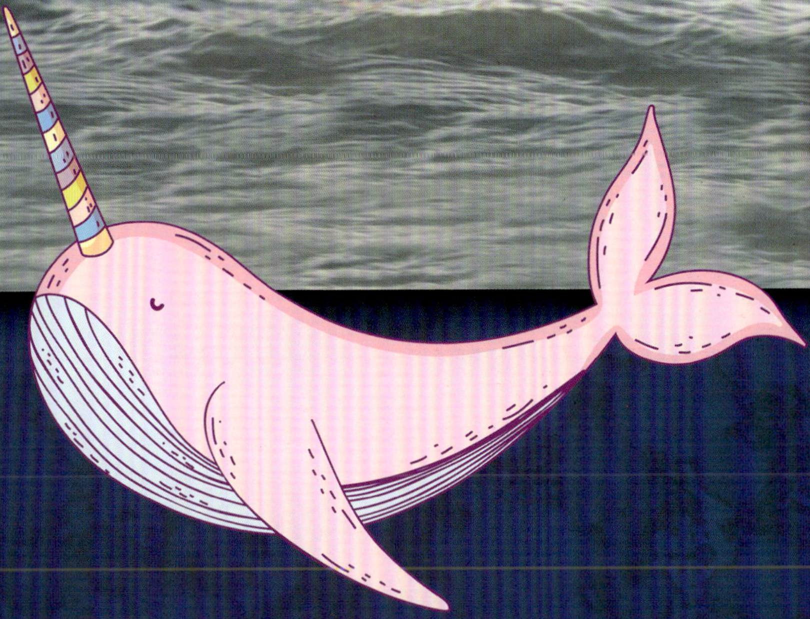

Symbols

In Europe, unicorns would come to symbolize, or stand for, love and faithfulness. They also symbolized power and **innocence**. The creature's goodness and ability to save others made it a symbol for Jesus Christ in stories and art.

IMAGINE THAT!

TAPESTRIES KNOWN AS "THE HUNT OF THE UNICORN" ARE EXAMPLES OF A UNICORN SYMBOLIZING JESUS IN ART.

Unicorn Hoax!

During the 1980s, some wondered if unicorns had finally been found! The Ringling Bros. and Barnum & Bailey Circus displayed them. No one knew how it was possible. The circus said the unicorns simply showed up one day.

IMAGINE THAT!

LATER, IT CAME OUT THAT A SPECIAL **SURGERY** DONE TO A GOAT SOON AFTER IT WAS BORN MADE IT ABLE TO GROW ONE, LARGE HORN.

Fantasy Books

Many of the most well-known fantasy book series feature unicorns, including *The Chronicles of Narnia*. A unicorn named Jewel fights against the evil queen in the series. In the *Harry Potter* books, unicorn hairs can be used to make wands.

IMAGINE THAT!

IN *HARRY POTTER*, DRINKING UNICORN BLOOD CAN KEEP SOMEONE ALIVE. HOWEVER, DOING SO WILL ALSO CURSE THE PERSON WHO DRINKS IT.

SPANISH-LANGUAGE VERSION OF *HARRY POTTER AND THE SORCERER'S STONE*, FEATURING A UNICORN

Pop Culture Unicorns

Unicorns are found beyond fantasy stories too! Rainicorns, a kind of rainbow and unicorn being, appeared in the TV show *Adventure Time*. In the card game Magic the Gathering, there have been more than 30 unicorn cards!

IMAGINE THAT!

POKÉMON ALSO FEATURES UNICORNS: RAPIDASH, GALARIAN PONYTA, AND GALARIAN RAPIDASH.

Unicorns Around the World

These are just some of the symbols and flags that have used unicorns around the world.

ROYAL COAT OF ARMS
of Scotland (until 1603)

ROYAL COAT OF ARMS
of the United Kingdom

FLAG OF SOROCABA
São Paulo, Brazil

FLAG OF BOGOTOL
town in Russia

FLAG OF THE PRESIDENT
of Lithuania

FOR MORE INFORMATION

BOOKS

Munsey, Lizzie, et al. *Supernatural Creatures: Mythical and Sacred Creatures from Around the World.* New York, NY: DK, 2024.

Nardo, Don. *Creatures and Beasts in World Mythology.* San Diego, CA: ReferencePoint Press, Inc., 2025.

WEBSITES

Fantasy Books for Kids
https://www.commonsensemedia.org/lists/fantasy-books-for-kids
Find lots of great fantasy books for kids here.

Fantasy Movies for Kids
https://www.commonsensemedia.org/lists/best-fantasy-movies
Find your next favorite fantasy movie here!

Publisher's note to educators and parents: Our editors have carefully reviewed these websites to ensure that they are suitable for students. Many websites change frequently, however, and we cannot guarantee that a site's future contents will continue to meet our high standards of quality and educational value. Be advised that students should be closely supervised whenever they access the internet.

GLOSSARY

ancient: Very old.

exist: To be real and living.

fantasy: Having to do with imaginative stories that feature impossible events and characters.

innocence: Having to do with being innocent, or one who is blameless and should not be harmed.

mythical: Having to do with myths, which are stories that were told by a people to explain a practice, belief, or natural event.

pop culture: Popular culture, or the interests of many people, including books and movies.

spiral: A shape that curls outward from a center point or inward towards a center point.

surgery: A medical treatment that involves cutting into the skin or other body tissue.

tapestry: A heavy reversible cloth woven by hand that often has pictures or designs on it.

INDEX